Wedding Toasts and Traditions

ISBN 0-939298-45-7

PRINTED IN THE UNITED STATES OF AMERICA

Author's Preface

Marriage as we know it is very different from marriage in former times. Until the Middle Ages, a king could marry his first cousin, a priest could have a wife and several concubines, and a nobleman could divorce his wife if she didn't produce a son. Marriage has often been used as a tool to gain political power, and until comparatively recently a woman often had no voice in choosing her husband.

Marriage has a long and complex history, some of which is in direct contrast to the modern way of thinking. In the interest of accuracy and completeness, I have included some customs which, by modern standards, are sexist, offensive, and crude. By the same token, however, the larger part of this material is interesting and relevant to our modern way of celebrating the wedding. Especially interesting to me is the way in which ancient or outmoded customs linger in the modern ceremony in the form of symbols. My interest in the symbolic aspects of wedding ceremonies is what led ultimately to the creation of this volume.

A special word needs to be said about toasting. As one of the oldest and most widespread customs, toasting holds a special place in a book like this. The practice of drinking a toast to the health of a friend or loved one on special occasions, often with wine or some other alcoholic beverage, should not be taken as an endorsement on my part of the consumption of alcohol. There are plenty of non-alcoholic beverages which are perfectly acceptable, and I encourage each of you to make your toast with the beverage of your choice.

Mark Ishee
June 1986

To my parents, without whose inspiration this book would not have been possible.

Contents

1

Origin and History of Marriage

Origin and History of Marriage

Without question, marriage is the oldest of social institutions. Universal in its scope, it has evolved through many forms before becoming what it is today.

Marriage by Decree

Marriage was instituted by God when he declared, "It is not good that man should be alone; I will make him a helper comparable to him" (Gen. 2:18). So God fashioned woman and brought her to man. On seeing the woman, Adam exclaimed, "This is now bone of my bones and flesh of my flesh; she shall be called Woman, because she was taken out of Man" (Gen. 2:23). This passage also emphasizes the truth that "a man shall leave his father and mother and be joined to his wife, and they shall become one flesh" (Gen. 2:24). This suggests that God's ideal is for man to be the husband of one wife and that this marriage is to be permanent.

The time span between God's decree and the beginning of recorded history is unknown. In tracing the origins of marriage customs, we find the marriage ceremony has progressed through three general stages: marriage by capture, marriage by purchase, and marriage by mutual love.

Marriage by Force

Our earliest records indicate that originally marriages were consummated by force, the groom capturing a desirable woman, often of another tribe. Although some writers have referred to this practice as a form of rape, it is actually a form of marriage. When primitive man stole a woman, he did so more often than not because he wanted a wife.

Primitive cultural and tribal groups were routinely hostile toward each other. Victory by one tribe over another was always followed by pillaging, and women were often captured and taken away by the conquering tribe. Primitive man no doubt preferred a captured wife to one from his own tribe. Not only was she a testament to his strength in warfare, she also helped to avoid the horrors of incest that often plagued primitive peoples. Throughout primitive life, warriors who married captive women were considered more honorably married than those who married from within their own tribe.

Disproportion among the sexes also led to marriage by capture. Many primitives practiced female infanticide, which of course led to a shortage of females within the tribe. The males of the tribe either fought among themselves for the available women or sought other women from different tribes.

The custom of having the "best man" in attendance at the wedding is a holdover from the days of marriage by capture. When a man sought to capture a wife from another tribe, he often brought along his "best man" to assist him. Thus, the "best man" is the modern counterpart of the fellow-warrior, who helped the bridegroom capture and carry away the bride.

Several cases of marriage by capture are mentioned in the Bible. For example, the tribe of Benjamin obtained wives for themselves by massacring the inhabitants of Jabez-Gilead and capturing four hundred virgins. On another occasion, the Benjamites captured women during a feast near Bethel. Yet another example is the vanquishing of the Midianites by the Israelites and the subsequent capture of all cattle, children, and women. Refer to Numbers 21:7-9, and also to Deuteronomy 21 for a complete description of marriage by capture as practiced by the Israelites.

It is also known that marriage by capture was once common in ancient Greece, and that the form was retained by the Spartans as an important aspect of the wedding ceremony. Even after Christianity abolished marriage by capture, the Anglo-Saxons persisted in simulating the capture of the bride in their marriage customs.

The honeymoon is a relic of the days of marriage by capture as well. Frequently the tribe from which a warrior stole a bride would come looking for her, and it was necessary for the warrior and his new wife to go into hiding to avoid being discovered. Thus, the honeymoon evolved as symbolic of the period of time during which the bridegroom hid until the bride's kinsmen grew tired of looking for her.

The symbol of capture as retained in later systems of marriage seems to be related to primitive notions of modesty and delicacy. In most cases, marriage was a change for the worse for the bride. Realizing this, often the bride would struggle and protest her capture. The screams, tears, and protests of the bride are considered essential among many cultures to show the bride's bashfulness and modesty. Even today, when marriage by capture is no longer widely practiced, it is customary in many parts of the world for the bride to indicate in one way or another that marriage is being forced upon her and that she is not entering it willingly.

Marriage by capture has left definite traces in modern marriage customs. Even though these remnants are symbolic, playful throwbacks, they demonstrate how recently marriage by capture was the rule and not the exception.

Marriage by Contract

It is not difficult to see how marriage by capture gradually gave way to marriage by contract, or marriage by purchase. Originally the two concepts must have represented one system of marriage. The bride was first stolen, and later compensation was provided to her family or tribe to escape their vengeance.

It would seem that the custom of purchasing a wife began with the desire to placate enraged parents, and also to avoid tribal warfare that might result if such compensation were not forthcoming.

In the earliest stages of marriage by purchase, an exchange was made instead of a price being paid. It is not difficult to envision circumstances in which this would occur. Imagine that a would-be bridegroom, having recently stolen his bride away from her family, is overtaken by her angry family and is ordered to pay for her. Unable to do so, he offers instead to exchange his own sister, his livestock, or his land for her. In this way he is able not only to save his own life but also to keep his freedom and his new wife.

The very word "wedding" betrays the great stage of wife purchase through which marriage passed. The *wed* was the money, horses, or cattle which the groom gave as security and as a pledge to prove his purchase of the bride from her father. From this *wed* we derive the idea of "wedding" or "pledging" the bride to the man who pays the required security for her.

However, even more common than the exchange of goods or land for the bride was the exchange of the groom's own labor for her. By rendering certain services to the bride's father, the groom could strike an elementary contract through which he would purchase his wife. This form of bridal purchase was most common among the uncivilized peoples of America, Africa, Asia, and India, and is also the basis of the Biblical story of Jacob and Rachel in the Old Testament.

Many early peoples developed the custom of giving valuable presents to the parents of the bride in return for their consent to her marriage. Until recently, in Japan it was customary for a young man who wished to marry to send presents both to her and to her parents. The type and value of the gifts was not left to the bridegroom himself, but was negotiated over a long period of time. The sending of such presents formed an important part of the marriage ceremony — once they had been sent and received, the marriage contract was sealed, and neither

14

party could withdraw. Of course, this is just another form of marriage by purchase, but it is closer in spirit to modern marriage methods than some of the other forms considered above. Similarly, among the North American Indians, it was customary for a young brave to present gifts not to the girl, but to her father. If the gifts were accepted, the betrothal was considered sealed.

The most common compensation for a bride in primitive life was property paid for her to her owner or owners. The price varied according to her health, her social rank, and so on. Among certain peoples, a widow often brought only half the price that the guardian or father of a maiden usually demanded.

In the earliest written laws on the subject, marriage consisted of two separate transactions. First, there was the agreement between the bridegroom and the bride's father or guardian, each formally binding himself to his part in the marriage agreement. Second, there was the delivery of the bride in return for the price agreed upon, or payment of part of the price and security that the remainder would be paid to the widow in case of the husband's untimely death. Here originated the custom of the dower (from the Italian *dos*) in the more advanced sense — a provision for widowhood. Instead of paying the agreed-upon fee to the father or guardian of the bride, it was paid to the bride herself as a sort of "life insurance" on her husband.

In Old Testament times, the parents chose the mate for their son. The primary reason for the parents' choosing the bride was that she became part of the clan. Although they were married and they became "one flesh," the couple remained under the jurisdiction of the bridegroom's father. The parents chose someone who would best fit into their clan and work harmoniously with her mother-in-law and sisters-in-law.

Even if the young wife lost her husband in war or accident, she remained within the clan and was wed to her brother-in-law or next of kin. This arrangement is called "levirate marriage," and is the basis for the story of Ruth and Boaz (see Ruth 3:13; 4:1-12; Deut. 25:5-10). Sometimes the parents consulted with the children to see if they approved of the choice being made for them. For example, Rebekah was asked if she wanted to marry Isaac (see Gen. 24:58). Samson, contrary to the norm, demanded that a certain girl be acquired for him. Although his parents protested, they completed the marriage contract for him.

Another reason why the parents made the choice was that the children were often married at a young age. In fact, by New Testament times, the Jewish leaders had decided to establish minimum ages for which a marriage contract could be drawn up. The age was set at thirteen for boys and twelve for girls.

The Mosaic Law clearly states that an Israelite was never to marry a Canaanite, for there would be a constant temptation to embrace the spouse's god as well (see Ex. 34:10-17; Deut. 7:3-4). Likewise, the Apostle Paul commanded the members of the church at Corinth: "Do not be unequally yoked together with unbelievers" (2 Cor. 6:14).

Marriages between Israelites were legislated and all incestuous relationships were outlawed (see Lev. 18:6-8; 20:19-21). In addition, priests were forbidden to marry prostitutes and divorced women (see Lev. 21:7, 13-14). Daughters who inherited their father's possessions had to marry within their tribe or lose their inheritance (see Num. 27:8; 36:2-4).

One of the most effective systems for wife purchase was created by the Babylonians. Twice a year, all girls of marriageable age were assembled in a space before the temple and offered for sale to the highest bidders, much like a modern auction. The most attractive girls brought large prices, and this money was turned over to the less attractive girls who had appeared at several such events and who seemed unlikely to attract a husband. The large sums of money became an attraction to would-be suitors, and in time every girl had a husband.

The ancient Scandinavians believed that even the gods bought their wives, a thought prevalent throughout mythology. Even so, abduction without payment was common, and necessitated that the couple remain in hiding until they were able to pay the bride's parent or guardian the required price or compensation.

Marriage by contract or purchase lasted in England as late as the middle of the sixteenth century. In France, it was customary up until the marriage of Louis XVI to pay thirteen deniers upon the conclusion of a marriage contract. Additionally, the practice of "giving the bride away" in the modern ceremony has its roots in the time when the bride was really sold.

Marriage by Mutual Love

Marriage by mutual love evolved gradually. Although romance prior to marriage is not unknown in Old Testament times, it played a minor role in the life of teenagers of that era; they did not marry one they "loved;" they "loved" the one they married. Love began at marriage; it may, but need not, precede marriage. When Isaac married Rebekah, Scripture records that "she became his wife, and he loved her" (Gen. 24:67).

It was not until the 9th or 10th century that women gained the privilege of choosing or refusing their husbands according to their own judgment. Rare exceptions to this are recorded since primitive times, where women claimed the right to select their mates, but the custom was not widespread until well into the 9th and 10th centuries.

From the many stories, legends, and myths that have come down to us from ages past, we know that love has always played a part in marriage. However, civilization had to advance beyond the primitive stages before marriage by love became accepted. In fact, the position of the woman within any given society forms an accurate gauge as to how far toward civilization that society has progressed. Whenever marriage by purchase falls into decay, then true civilization begins. On the other hand, a culture which practices marriage by capture is in the lowest stages of barbarism. In modern civilized life, marriage by capture occurs only as a symbol, and marriage by contract occurs rarely. Marriage through mutual love is the hallmark of a civilized people.

Egypt, one of the earliest civilizations, honored and respected women. At various times Egypt was ruled by several queens, and surviving works of art from ancient Egypt leave no doubt that women were for the most part on an equal footing with men.

The practice of elopement, often wrongly interpreted as a throwback to the days of marriage by capture, is in fact one of the most obvious expressions of marriage by mutual love. In primitive times, elopement was almost impossible: women were guarded too closely. Parents and guardians arranged marriage to suit their own greedy ends, without thought for the desires or the ultimate happiness of the bride-to-be.

Thus, elopement gradually emerged as the only viable alternative to marriage by capture or by purchase. Arising spontaneously in numerous cultures, it always was at first a rarity, then became more and more common as time passed. To avoid marrying a man she disliked but who was able to pay the price her parents demanded, a young woman would decide to elope with the man of her choice. Also, in order to avoid having to wait until he could pay the bride-price, or to escape having to work for her under a service contract, a young man would often induce the girl he loved to elope with him.

It was not nearly as easy in former times as it is today to elope. In a society which regarded daughters as salable possessions, and therefore a source of profit, it was not usually possible to be forgiven for eloping. The young couple had to elope to a far-away land, probably without a source of livelihood, and begin life anew away from their people. In contrast, elopement is today looked upon with toleration and even with approval in circumstances where parental objection seems to be unfounded.

The Evolution of Modern Marriage

There was a period of time during the Roman Republic when the marriage ceremony was a solemn religious ordinance. Later, however, religion fell into contempt and marriage became virtually a civil contract. By slow degrees, Christianity gave marriage back its religious character as couples paired off together to ask for the blessing of their pastor. By the Middle Ages, the religious aspect of marriage had become most significant. The priest was even called in to bless the marriage bed! The custom of religious marriage, performed in the church or by a clergyman in the home, became widespread during the Middle Ages and survives to this day.

It was not until the Council of Trent in 1563 that the Catholic church made it mandatory for a marriage to be performed by a priest in the presence of two or three witnesses. Subsequently, marriage continued to be regarded as a divine institution until the French Revolution, when the new Constitution made civil marriage mandatory in 1791.

Christianity dealt a death blow to marriage by purchase by advocating a more wholesome and civilized attitude toward women and toward marriage. Old habits and traditions die hard, however, and it was many generations before the civilized world had rid itself of wife purchase and woman barter.

The modern marriage, regardless of sect, has a more solemn and religious tone because of the impact of Christianity. Despite this religious character, however, shreds of the old customs remain in the popular memory. Outmoded traditions resurface as symbols, blending the old with the new and making modern marriages as colorful and romantic as any that have gone before.

2

Traditions

Traditions

"Something old, something new, something borrowed, something blue"

Nearly all of our wedding traditions have been borrowed from past cultures. It was the ancient Hebrews who first encouraged brides to wear blue ribbons on their wedding days. They considered the color blue to be symbolic of love, purity, and fidelity. Wearing something borrowed from a happily married woman was thought to transfer her wedded bliss to the new bride.

Old Testament Customs

A number of customs and steps were involved in finalizing a marriage in Old Testament times. The first was agreeing on a price to be given to the father of the girl. The payment was compensation for the loss of a worker. The sum was mutually agreed upon (see Gen. 34:12; Ex. 22:16-17) and could include services instead of money. For example, Jacob agreed to work for seven years for Rachel (see Gen. 29:18-20). The giving and receiving of money was probably accompanied by a written agreement. Hereafter, the couple was engaged.

In biblical times, a betrothal for marriage was a binding agreement which set the young woman apart for the young man. The agreement was voided only by death or divorce; one could not get out of the betrothal in any other way. When Joseph discovered that Mary was pregnant, he did not want to make a "public example" of her; instead, he decided to divorce her secretly. However, he did not carry out the divorce because an angel of the Lord convinced him that the baby to be born to Mary would be the Son of God (see Matt. 1:18-25).

During the engagement period, the bridegroom had certain privileges. If war was declared, he was exempt from military duty (see Deut. 20:17). Also, he knew that his bride-to-be was protected by Mosaic Law. If another man raped his fiancée, the act was treated as adultery and punished accordingly (see Deut. 22:23-27). This was considered a more serious crime than the rape of a girl not yet betrothed (see Deut. 22:28-29).

The time of engagement varied. Sometimes the couple was married the same day that they were engaged. Usually, however, a period of time elapsed between the betrothal and the marriage ceremony. During this time the young man prepared living accommodations in his father's house for his bride. The bride prepared herself for married life.

On the day that the wedding was to take place, the groom and his friends dressed in their finest clothes and together went to the home of the bride (see Song of Solomon 3:6-11). Together the couple went back to the groom's house. Their friends sang and danced their way back to his house.

Once at the groom's house, the couple was ushered into a bridal chamber. The marriage was consummated as the guests waited outside. Once that fact was announced, the wedding festivities continued, with guests dropping by and feasting on the food that had been prepared. Usually the wedding party lasted for a week; however, on occasions they lasted for two weeks (Gen. 29:27).

WEDDING RING CUSTOMS

The Engagement Ring

The gift of a ring is a very old tradition which was used to seal any important or sacred agreement (Gen. 10:41-42). A Greek engagement or betrothal ring of the fourth century B.C. bears the inscription: "To her who excels not only in virtue and prudence, but also in wisdom."

The popularity of the diamond as an engagement stone stems from the superstition that its sparkle comes from the fires of love.

The Wedding Ring

Before the engagement and wedding rings came into being, a man and his intended wife would break a piece of gold or silver in half. The man kept one half and the woman the other. That meant they were engaged to be married.

Primitive man, who wove a cord and bound it around the waist of a woman he wanted, believed that her spirit entered his body when this was done, and that she was bound to him forever. These circlets of rushes or hemp had to be replaced every year.

Rings as symbols of authority have come down to us through the ages. The wedding ring is believed to have evolved from the engagement ring. Wedding rings were given in the days of marriage by purchase both as partial payment and as a symbol of the prospective groom's good intentions. The early Assyrians, Hebrews, Greeks, and Romans all used the signet ring as a means of sealing documents and as a means of transferring authority or ownership.

Some believe that the wedding ring is simply the miniature of the fetters placed on the girl's hands and feet during the days when brides were captured rather than wooed. According to this belief, the use of the circular shape as symbolic of eternity developed much later.

A ring has been used to signify union since the days of the early Egyptians. Their literature mentions rings in connection with weddings, and it is likely that the first "wedding rings" were used by the Egyptians. The circle of the ring represents mutual love and affection roundly flowing from one to the other. The circle represented eternity in Egyptian hieroglyphic script, and marriage was seen as a permanent bond.

The very shape of the wedding ring is symbolic of the intentions of both parties to uphold their marriage vows forever. Some authorities connect the round shape of the ring with the idea of completeness: many ancient peoples believed that a man without a woman is half a man, and a woman without a man is half a woman.

Wedding rings have been considered essential to the wedding ceremony since ancient times. Many facts have been recorded concerning the ring and the part it has played in various marriage systems. One amusing incident concerns a duke who was in a hurry to marry his lady: the parson insisted on a ring to make the marriage valid, so the duke borrowed the ring from the bed curtain.

Affluent cultures have long favored the lasting beauty and purity of gold for their wedding bands, but the earliest pledge rings were made of braided grass, while later ones were fashioned of leather, carved stone and crude metals. Ancient wedding rings were made of everything from rush and bone to jet, gold, iron, and silver. The diamond was incorporated into engagement rings by Italians during the Middle Ages. They chose the most imperishable of all stones as a symbol of enduring love.

Long after the Norman Conquest, English peasants used rings made of rush because they could afford none better. Among the Jewish people the ring was first introduced in the eighth century A.D. to replace the tradition of handing the bride a small coin as a "promissory note" of the husband's ability to meet all future financial obligations toward his wife.

In early times there was no customary size for a wedding ring. Usually the ring was fashioned to suit the means, rather than the tastes, of the lovers in question. Some rings were large and heavy, while others were very small. They differed as much in size and shape as they did in the materials from which they were made.

According to tradition, early Hebrew wedding rings were usually plain gold, silver, or base metal without any setting. Apparently, Jewish wedding rings were of a ceremonial nature because they were often too large to wear on the finger.

The Hebrews and the Greeks both used very large, heavy rings. The Romans customarily used a heavy iron ring, and it was customary also among the Romans to give the keys to the house with the bridal ring. Sometimes the ring and the keys were joined together. The Greeks made very elaborate rings, and often decorated them with engraved seals or adorned them with precious stones. In Iceland, a large ring of bone, jet, stone, gold, or silver was used, and was sometimes so large as to allow a person's entire hand to be passed through it. The Icelandic groom would extend his hand through one side of the ring, and his bride would do likewise from the other side. Hands joined thus, the marriage became finalized.

Many cultures evolved the tradition of breaking the wedding ring in two, each partner keeping half, as a means of identifying the other in case of prolonged absence.

The use of wedding rings among Christians has been traced back to the year A.D. 860. It is said that when a marriage settlement was properly sealed, rings bearing the names of the newly-married couple were passed around for inspection among the guests.

In Shakespeare's time it was customary to engrave the wedding ring. As many as three or four lines of verse were inscribed, in letters so small they could scarcely be read. The point of this tradition was to provide a permanent record of the marriage. For this purpose, many mottos for bridal rings were created, for example: "I will be yours while life endures;" and "In thee my choice do I rejoice." The tradition of engraving bits of religious wisdom upon wedding rings began to appear about this time also in Jewish marriages, and the practice of engraving some sort of saying inside the wedding ring continued into the 17th century, during which almost every ring was inscribed.

The plain gold wedding band became popular among the English-speaking peoples after Queen Mary's time, and gradually spread throughout Europe as the conventional choice. This tradition dates back as far as 1554 to Queen Mary's marriage to Philip of Spain, prior to which there was a dispute as to the nature of the ring to be used. Mary herself settled the argument (possibly for all time!) by declaring that she would prefer a simple ring unadorned with gems, for "she chose to be wedded with a plain hoop of gold, like other maidens."

The wedding ring is placed on the third finger of the left hand because it was believed that this finger is connected directly to the heart by the "vena amoris," or vein of love. But most fingers of both hands, including the thumb, have been used for wedding rings in the past. During the Elizabethan period in England, the wedding ring was worn on the thumb, as is shown in oil paintings of ladies of that time. In traditional Jewish weddings, the ring is placed on the first finger of the left hand.

In popular superstition, the right hand symbolizes power and authority, the left hand, subjection. It is often said that the ring is worn on the left hand to symbolize the subjection of the wife to the husband. There is no proof that this is the case, but it is a logical deduction given that the history of marriage has often involved women in roles inferior to those of their husbands.

The English Prayer Book of 1549 specified the left hand as the ring hand for both bride and groom. Since then it has become the tradition for all English-speaking people to wear the wedding band and engagement ring on the third finger of the left hand.

In ancient church ritual the ring was placed first on the thumb, "in the Name of the Father;" next on the forefinger, "in the Name of the Son;" then on the middle finger, "and of the

Holy Spirit." It was placed last on the third finger, "Amen," and left there as a seal of the marriage bond.

Some women refuse to remove their wedding rings after they have been placed on their fingers.

Bridal Shower

It is believed that the first bridal shower took place in Holland when a maiden fell in love with a poor miller. Her father forbade the marriage, but the miller's friends "showered" the bride with gifts so she would be able to marry without the benefit of the traditional dowry which helped most brides set up housekeeping.

Years later, an Englishwoman heard of a good friend who was to be married and wanted to give her a gift to express her congratulations. But the gift seemed too small. Remembering the story of the Dutch girl and the miller, she called the bride's friends and suggested they present their gifts at the same time. The party was so successful that others tried it, and bridal showers have been held ever since.

The Eskimo women say that bridal showers are an invention of the white man and his culture. The Eskimos celebrate after the wedding. Before a couple marry they make sure they have enough money to get buckets of candy. As soon as the marriage ceremony is ended, everyone is given large amounts of candy. Then a feast is enjoyed with lots of Eskimo food — caulk (frozen raw fish), seal blubber, and seal oil are among the favorite dishes.

Gifts for the Bride

Gifts for the bride are similar today to those of past years. During the reign of Maximilian, Archduke of Austria in 1477, common gifts for the bride were jewelry, tableware, bedding, and clothing.

29

In olden days in Japan, upon marriage a girl's mother presented her with a small dagger in a beautiful little case. This was not, as we might suppose, for the purpose of knifing her husband if he displeased her; rather, it was designed for the bride to use upon herself rather than come home crying to mama if the marriage did not succeed.

Proposal

Sometimes a young man proposed to a girl by giving her a pair of gloves. If the girl wore them to church, that meant she had accepted the proposal. Why gloves? Who knows? Maybe because the word "glove" contains the word "love."

Courtship

Many cultures of our world decry courtship as we know it in the United States. Their children do not choose their mates; the parents choose for them. This is done very carefully, considering the family background of a potential mate, his financial situation, similarities in social status, and agreement in religion.

The Hope Chest

The idea of the "hope chest" grew out of the ancient tradition of the dowry, which in turn grew out of the much older custom of marriage by purchase (see Chapter 1). In olden times, girls were expected to enter marriage with hope chests full of useful and beautiful articles for their future homes. A prospective bridegroom had the right to inspect his intended's hope chest and to call off the wedding if it did not meet with his approval.

The Trousseau

The word trousseau originated from the word trusse, meaning a little bundle.

Circumcision

There is undoubtedly magic significance to the importance of circumcision not only among the Jews, Moslems, and some members of Christian sects, but also among the natives of the West Coast of Africa, the Kafirs, the aborigines of Australia, nearly all the peoples of Eastern and Central Africa, Madagascar, Melanesia, the Indian Archipelago, Polynesia, and many of the Indian tribes of the Western Hemisphere. Circumcision is conceded to be the oldest surgical operation, and it is the only one still having a religious significance, or considered to be a prerequisite to marriage.

Bundling

Bundling was an old New England tradition introduced by the Dutch and the English which permitted engaged couples to lie together in bed without undressing during long, cold winter evenings.

Spooning

In Wales, a man would often carve a spoon from a piece of wood with his pocket knife. This would be attached to a ribbon and worn by a girl around her neck as a sign of their engagement. The expression "spooning" meaning to court or go steady originated from this tradition.

The Marriage Season

Nowadays, the wedding is a year-round event, but in former times certain seasons of the year were designated as the traditional time for marriage. In Morocco, marriages are generally celebrated in autumn at the close of the harvest season, when graineries are full of corn. But most European countries follow the Roman practice of holding weddings in Spring, when homage was paid to the three major divinities: Ceres, Maia, and Flora. May is traditionally an unlucky month for marriage, perhaps because in Roman folklore it was the month of old men. June has always been a popular month for weddings, and in Roman culture June was dedicated to Juno, goddess of young people.

The Bachelor Dinner

This tradition is believed to have originated in Sparta, where the bridegroom entertained his friends at supper on the eve of the wedding. This event was known as the "men's mess." Today this event is usually called a "bachelor party," and often features bawdy entertainment. However, the bachelor party is slowly giving way to the co-ed bride-and-groom shower, in which the bride and groom and their friends celebrate the up-coming wedding together.

The Bridal Wreath

The custom of wearing a wreath of orange blossoms was introduced in Europe by the Crusaders. Orange blossoms were also carried by brides in their bouquets as a symbol of fertility. In Norway the bride always wears a wreath of white flowers. After the wedding ceremony she is blindfolded and surrounded by a circle of bridesmaids. She then dances a folk dance alone and gives the wreath to one of the maids, who according to legend will be the first to wed. The wreath is passed to each bridesmaid who then steps out of the circle. The game ends when the last bridesmaid receives the wreath.

Reception

In virtually all societies, some sort of feast accompanies the wedding ceremony. They last anywhere from a few minutes to a week or more.

In the Western world, weddings are almost always followed by a reception, which is the traditional time to receive and acknowledge the married couple, to toast them, share their joy, and see them off on their honeymoon. In many past cultures, however, the wedding ceremony and the reception have been combined into one celebration. People feasted with the couple even as the wedding ceremony was taking place, and for many primitive peoples, the wedding was the feast. Only later did the two evolve into separate events.

Eating and drinking together is one of the oldest signs of love and union. Primitive man most likely shared food and drink with his mate, and considered that they were united by simple sharing. The Ancient Hebrews made drinking wine a part of their marriage service, and it is not hard to see the symbolism behind it. Such sharing is universal, and is as old as man himself.

The sharing between bride and groom naturally extends to the wedding guests. The communal aspect of the wedding is very important, for it is the way the couple shares their new happiness with their friends and family.

In primitive times, wedding parties consisted of the entire clan, tribe, or village. A wedding was an occasion for singing, dancing, and celebration. In many societies, rules and laws were relaxed. People could drink openly to excess without reprisal, and sexual customs were relaxed. In some societies, sexual intercourse was permitted even between strangers, although outlawed at normal times. The feast often went on for days, until the participants collapsed from exhaustion.

As social customs became more sophisticated and regulated, the wedding "feast" became a "reception" where the bride and groom could meet with friends and family. The reception is similar to the feast, but the activities are much milder in comparison. Receiving lines are now customary, so that the couple can meet the guests in an orderly fashion. Most of the wild rituals have been replaced or made acceptable by modern standards, but the reception itself remains an important part of the wedding.

Wedding Cake

Dating back to antiquity, the traditional white, frosted wedding cake is an updated version of the grain cake. It has always been a "special" food, at least symbolically, because it is communal: everyone eats from it, both as a sign of union and also as a way of wishing luck to the newly-married couple. When the bride and groom slice the first piece of wedding cake and offer it to each other, they are carrying on one of man's oldest rituals.

The modern wedding cake is probably directly descended from the Roman *conferreratio*, a particular kind of cake which was broken on the bride's head as a symbol of fruitfulness, plenty, and good fortune. Guests scrambled for the fragments of cake that fell, hoping to get in on some of the luck themselves. This tradition continues today with what is called the groom's cake, which is neatly boxed for guests to take home with them from the reception.

A modern-day custom is to remove the small top layer of the wedding cake and keep it in the freezer, to be shared by the couple on their first anniversary.

The Kiss

The Scotch in particular were greatly impressed with the importance of the bridal kiss. According to one old Scottish source, "the parson who presided over the marriage ceremony uniformly claimed it as his inaniable privilege to have a smack at the lips of the bride immediately after the performance of his official duties."

The Dollar Dance

In some communities, guests who dance with the bride or groom at the reception are required to pay a dollar for each dance. A variation of this custom is for guests to put money or checks in a small white satin purse the bride wears on her wrist.

Throwing Shoes

The Assyrians and Hebrews gave a sandal as a token of good faith when closing a bargain or to signify the transfer of property. The Egyptians exchanged sandals to indicate a transfer of property or granting authority. It was customary to fling a sandal to the ground as a symbol of possession of the land (see Psalms 60:8; 108:9).

In old Britain it was customary for the father to give his new son-in-law one of the bride's shoes, in token of the transfer of authority, and the bride was tapped on the head with the shoe to impress her with her husband's new authority and position. However, the husband was obliged to take an oath to treat his wife well. Shoes have also been thrown away by the bride's parents as a symbol that they have renounced their authority over their daughter.

Decorating Cars

Old shoes trailing the bridal get-away car is a dying custom, but signs, balloons, and streamers are still popular. This tradition is supposed to bring luck to the newlyweds.

Drop the Handkerchief

The game "Drop the Handkerchief" was originally designed not for children but for a young man who wished to propose to a young lady by dropping a handkerchief behind her.

The Other Half

The term "the other half" stems from an early Greek superstition. The Greeks believed that when a man fell in love with a woman and married her, he was simply being reunited with the half of himself that had been severed from him earlier by a supernatural power. Love at first sight proved he had found his "other half," later to be dubbed "the better half."

Tying the Knot

Calling marriage "tying the knot" stems from ancient times. The Danish used to tie two pieces of cord or ribbon together in the marriage ceremony to signify the couple's becoming one. Later that custom spread to Holland and England, and we still use the term "tying the knot" today.

Best Man

While friends of the bridal couple are intent on mischief at the wedding, the best man's duty is to help the groom and his bride escape their tricks. This custom goes back to early times when a young man captured his bride by force. While the couple made their getaway, the groom's friend fought off protesting relatives (see Chapter 1).

Honeymoon

The honeymoon (literally "moon of honey," from the French *lune de miel*) originated during the era of marriage by capture. The bridal couple hid for a month or so until the angry relatives gave up looking for them (see Chapter 1). During that time, according to an old French custom, as the moon went through all its phases the couple drank a wine made with honey called *metheglin*; hence, honeymoon. Many couples still keep their honeymoon plans a secret even if they are not afraid of being pursued by relatives.

In some cultures, a honeymoon consisted of the bride and groom being secluded in a house for a number of days and not allowed to come out or receive guests.

Today's honeymoons are usually shorter than a whole month, not only because of the expense but also because the couple frequently must return to work shortly after the wedding. Many modern couples choose weekend honeymoons.

3

Symbols

Symbols

The modern marriage ceremony is rife with symbolism, much of which is traceable to the early days of marriage by capture or by contract. Early Hebrew influences are evident. The Greek and Roman cultures, two of the most notable influences on modern western civilization, also have left remnants of their now-defunct culture in modern marriage symbolism. Early Christian weddings also have contributed to the modern wedding ceremony. Modern weddings often have a distinctively "medieval" tone, a holdover from Medieval England and France, where marriage as we know it originated.

Veils

Veils have a long and complicated history. The practice of covering the bride's face on her wedding day is widespread, and is recorded in numerous societies around the world. The first veils were worn as a superstition, protecting the bride from the "evil eye" of jealous rivals. The woman was regarded as weaker and more prone to danger. Greek and Roman brides wore flame-colored veils. Anglo-Saxon brides hid their blushes behind their own flowing tresses. This tradition lingered for centuries and became a common practice. Early Christian brides, who wore white or purple veils, changed the symbolism of it to represent youth and virginity, and it is in this form that the modern custom continues.

Among various ancient peoples, it was customary to keep the bride hidden from her future husband until the day of the wedding. In Egypt, for example, the groom was not permitted to look upon his bride's face until the wedding day, at which time he went through the solemn ceremony of uncovering her face. This same sort of ritual prevailed among the Arabs, Hindus, and various other European and Asiatic peoples.

In Moslem countries, women have always been regarded as servants, and until recently kept their faces veiled most of the time throughout their whole lives, since only her husband is supposed to see a woman's uncovered face. In this case, the veil is a symbol of submission and servitude. Many anthropologists believe that the wedding veil also had its origins in this attitude of male domination.

Wedding veils have also been used in some cultures to hide the face of the bride from the groom, especially where marriages were negotiated in childhood and the bride and groom never saw each other at all until after the wedding. After the marriage ceremony was complete, the husband would lift the veil and see his wife's face for the first time. Other cultures carried the practice to even greater lengths, to the extent of veiling the entire body. In some Eastern countries, a curtain was placed between the couple throughout the ceremony so that they could not see or touch each other until the wedding was concluded. These customs, originating in superstition, gave rise to the belief that it was bad luck for the bride and groom to see each other on the wedding day prior to the ceremony. Some cultures went so far as to separate the engaged couple for days or weeks before the event.

Nelly Custis began the veil fashion in this country when she chose to wear a lengthy scarf pinned to her coiffure at her wedding to President Washington's aide, Major Lawrence Lewis. Her decision stemmed from the flattering comments her fiancé made after glimpsing her through a lace curtain at an open window.

Giving the Bride Away

The bride is given away because in early times she was

looked on almost as chattel. Her parents arranged her marriage and she was literally given to the groom. Today, a woman is considered under her father's care until she is married. To signify his approval, the father walks to the altar with his daughter and gives her in marriage.

Wearing White

Why does the bride wear white? The early Romans wore white on their sacred days to denote purity. The church has always considered white a festival color emblematic of purity.

Flowers

Ancient Roman brides carried bunches of herbs under their wedding veils as symbols of fertility and fidelity. The Saracens chose orange blossoms; they were considered the flowers of fertility and happiness because the orange tree blooms and bears fruit at the same time. Lilies have long been symbols of purity, and roses the flower of love. Hence, June, the month of roses, is a popular wedding month. Ivy, used at early Greek weddings as a sign of indissoluble love, is still used to trim wedding bouquets.

Flower Girl

The flower girl's role in the wedding dates from the Middle Ages. Two little girls, usually sisters, dressed alike and carried wheat before the bride in the marriage procession, symbolizing the wish that the marriage would be fruitful. Later, flowers replaced the wheat, and it became customary to strew the flowers on the ground before the bride.

Blue

The brides of Israel in ancient times wore a blue ribbon on the border of their fringed robes to denote purity, fidelity, and love. Blue is also associated with the purity of the Virgin Mary.

The Wedding Gown

The bridal gown as we know it today was first introduced by Empress Eugenie, a leader of fashion. She wore the white gown at her wedding to Napoleon III, who ruled France from 1853 to 1871.

Wedding Presents

According to an etiquette book published in 1907 by the New York Society of Self-Culture, "Wedding presents have now, in some instances, become almost gorgeous. The old fashion started amongst the frugal Dutch with the custom of providing the young couple with their household gear and sum of money with which to begin their married life. It has now degenerated into a very bold display of wealth and ostentatious generosity, so that friends of moderate means are afraid to send anything." One of the most common methods of giving wedding gifts in modern times is through bridal registries, which provide friends and relatives with a range of choices (and prices!), and help to avoid duplication.

The French have more sensible customs about wedding presents — the nearest of kin subscribe a sum of money which is sent to the bride's mother, who invests it in good securities, in gold and silver, in the bridal trousseau, or in the furnishing of the house, as the good sense of all the parties combines to direct.

At the Altar

The reason why the bride traditionally stands to the left of the groom at the altar is symbolic of the now-defunct practice of marriage by capture. After the ceremony, the groom places her hand within his left arm to follow the clergyman into the vestry to sign the register. Finally, on the way out, the bride passes down the aisle, once again on the left arm of the bridegroom. She stands to his left and holds his left arm during these proceedings not to honor her, but to secure her. It enables the groom to keep his right (sword) hand free to defend her from attack and capture by jealous rivals.

Throwing the Bouquet

Years ago, a bride did not throw her bouquet, but permitted guests to scramble for her garter to obtain good luck! A bit disconcerting for the bride, to be sure. One young bride, hoping to avoid the tussle, took off and tossed her stocking instead. For a time that custom prevailed, until a bride who wanted to keep both garter and stocking decided to throw her bouquet instead. Various objects have been thrown by brides in the past, with the idea that the person who caught it would be the next to marry. It is traditionally the bride's way of wishing luck to the unmarried girls in the crowd.

4

Superstitions

Superstitions

Some of the world's greatest thinkers have been slaves to superstition. Sir Walter Scott had a dread of ghosts. Napoleon was afraid of black cats. Peter the Great had a superstitious fear of crossing bridges. Cotton Mather, noted American author and clergyman, participated in the Salem witch trials. Blackstone, upon whose work English law is founded, openly declared his belief in witches, a view shared by many notable lawyers and ministers of his day.

Few persons, no matter how rational, are not given to superstition of some sort. Many of our modern customs are "leftovers" of outmoded superstitious beliefs. Though known to be ineffective, many superstitious practices are carried forth from generation to generation. Many superstitions about love, courtship, and weddings are still widely practiced, if not believed, and a few have become a permanent part of our modern culture.

Good Luck Symbols

Most brides like to follow the superstition that they must wear "something old, something new, something borrowed, and something blue" for good luck. This custom originated with ancient Israelite brides, who were instructed to wear garments bordered with the color blue, which represented purity, love, and fidelity.

Legend says that Eve brought a four-leaf clover with her from the Garden of Eden, and that to have one in your own garden will bring good fortune. It once was customary to strew four-leaf clovers before the bride to insure her happiness in marriage.

Another popular good-luck custom is to distribute sugar-coated almonds to all guests. This souvenir, called *confetti* by Italians, represents the bitterness and sweetness of life. The almonds are attractively wrapped in tulle and tied with a ribbon.

Teasing

Because it was considered dangerous for lovers to be happy, it became customary to tease the bride and groom, to hide their belongings, and to be the targets for friendly abuse.

A good example of this teasing is still practiced today with the *shivaree*. The shivaree is a noisy mock serenade held late during the wedding night to harass the newlyweds. This early Latin custom was introduced in America by the French people of Canada and Louisiana.

The Wedding Veil

The wedding veil was originally designed to hide the bride from a jealous person who wanted to cast a spell upon her by giving her the "evil eye." It was also supposedly a protection against evil spirits, keeping them from knowing who she was. The Romans believed that demon spirits were jealous of people's happiness, and since weddings are joyful events, it was necessary to confuse the devil. Thus, Roman brides wore veils to throw the devil off the track (see Chapter 3).

Over the Threshold

Carrying the bride over the threshold symbolizes the

groom's conquest by force, as in the days of marriage by capture. Carrying a bride over the threshold of the new home was a precaution the Romans devised to prevent her either from tripping or from entering with her left foot, both of which they thought would have been disastrous to the marriage.

Wedding Attendants

The custom of having wedding attendants in the bridal party has its origin in superstition. It was formerly believed that having the attendants all dressed similarly to the bridal couple would confuse the evil spirits so they would not know which ones were being married. An old Roman custom dictated that every wedding have at least ten witnesses.

Taboos

One marriage taboo was that the bride should not see or talk to the groom before the ceremony on the day of the wedding. This practice is often ignored today.

Crying

In olden times the bride was supposed to cry when the groom kissed her during the wedding ceremony as a safeguard against a marriage full of tears. As mentioned in Chapter 1, this custom has its roots in the days of marriage by capture, when many brides entered marriage unwillingly.

Throwing Rice

Traditionally, people throw rice at the departing couple. Throwing rice, grain, or nuts at a wedding is one of the oldest superstitions, and has its roots in fear of evil spirits. The groom was sure that evil spirits were jealous of him, and must be appeased. The rice was designed to distract their attention from the bridal couple.

Confetti or bird seed are the modern inexpensive substitutes for the rice, wheat, or nuts originally thrown on newlyweds. Since most churches prohibit these materials to be thrown inside, it is most common to throw bird seed at the newlyweds outdoors as they depart. Bird seed is most often used because it does not have to be cleaned up later, and will not harm birds. Rice, on the other hand, will absorb water and puff up, killing any birds who have eaten it.

Grains that sustain life symbolically represent life and growth. A good crop is occasion for much joy. In the days before pregnancy and birth were understood, primitive man fashioned myths about the appearance of new life, both from the earth and from the womb. To the primitive mind, both were mysterious events involving risk and possible fatality. Thus, the superstition of throwing rice symbolizes the primitive association between woman and the life-bearing grain. Just as sowing seeds in the earth might make it fertile, so might throwing grain increase the bride's fertility. Since in many cultures a woman could be divorced or even killed for failing to bear children, throwing grain came to represent a wish for her good luck.

Other meanings of this ritual are known. The ancient Chinese threw rice, their symbol of health and prosperity, to insure the bridal couple's having many children. Among Indians, throwing rice, a basic food source, at the couple was a wish for their plenty and prosperity.

Rice and grains are not all that have been thrown at newlyweds. In many lands, eggs (obvious symbols of fertility) are thrown at the couple. Moroccans have the rather messy custom of the groom's throwing an egg at his new wife in the hope that she will have ease in child-bearing. Dates, figs, and other sweets have been thrown at newlyweds in order to sweeten their relationship. The Ancient Hebrews threw barley in front of the couple to represent their hope for numerous off-spring.

SUPERSTITIONS ABOUT
LOVE, COURTSHIP, AND WEDDINGS

Wedding Superstitions

If you marry on a Wednesday, you will be happy; if you marry or Friday or Saturday, you will be unhappy.

A double wedding means unhappiness to one of the couples.

It is bad luck to try on the wedding gown before the ceremony.

Losing the wedding ring brings bad luck.

The bride should step over the church sill with her right foot to assure happiness.

Valentine's Day Superstitions

Many girls hope to find their mates on Valentine's Day. According to superstition, at midnight on Valentine's Day Eve a girl should walk alone to a cemetery, carrying a handful of hemp seed. At the stroke of midnight she should scatter the hemp seed, sing a special song and run home, fully expecting to see her true love following her. She is sure to be married to him within a year.

On the eve of Valentine's Day, if a girl wants to find out who her husband will be, she should hard-boil an egg, replacing all the yolk with salt, and eat it, shell and all. She then should go to bed without speaking or drinking, expecting that the first man she sees the next morning will be her future husband.

How To Catch a Man

Pull a hair from the head of someone you love, and he will love you deeply.

He will love you if your serve him one of these potions:

- a bowl of soup with three drops of your blood in it

- a glass of lemonade that contains your fingernail filings or has had your toenail clippings soaked in it (remove toenails before serving).

Sure signs your marriage will take place soon:

- you stumble going up a flight of stairs

- you have hairy legs

- the lines on your palm form an M

- you dream of taking a bath

- you sit on a table

To discover your future mate's name:

- tag dry onions with boys' names before planting them. The first one that sprouts will be the man you will marry.

- fill your mouth with water, run around the block three times, and the first person you see after you stop will have the same name as your future husband.

To dream what your future husband will look like:

sleep with a mirror under your pillow;

count nine stars each night for nine nights;

wear your nightgown inside out;

rub your bedposts with lemon peels before turning off your lights.

To discover your future mate's initial:

soak a shoelace in water, throw it at the ceiling, and read the initial in the mark on the ceiling.

To marry anyone you choose:

eat one hundred chicken gizzards at one time, or swallow whole the raw heart of a chicken.

5

Information About Toasting

Information About Toasting

Toasting comes from an ancient French custom of putting a piece of bread in the bottom of a glass. Placing a piece of toasted bread in a tankard before ale or wine was poured into it was done to improve the taste by soaking up sediment and impurities in the bottom of the vessel. A good toaster drained the drink to get the "toast." Thus, the term "drinking a toast" originated, and subsequently evolved into the practice of drinking to a person's health.

When to Toast

Wedding toasts are usually proposed either at the reception or at the rehearsal dinner. In the former case, toasting begins immediately after the wedding meal is finished, or just after the cake-cutting ceremony. However, it is appropriate to propose a toast at any time after the receiving line has disbanded. In the latter case, toasting begins after dinner, at the discretion of the Master of Ceremonies.

Which Beverage?

The basic format for toasting is quite simple. Everyone present — guests as well as the wedding party — is served a beverage. Champagne or wine are the traditional drinks for toasts, but there is nothing wrong or improper about drinking a toast with non-alcoholic fruit punch, ginger ale, or white grape juice if alcoholic drinks are disapproved of or are inappropriate. Never use tea, coffee, or water when toasting.

Serving

When there is a head table, the beverage for the toast is first served to the bride, then to the groom, and then to the maid of honor, followed by the other guests seated at the head table. The best man is always the last person to receive a beverage. If there is no head table, the wedding party usually forms into a group to which beverages are served as soon as the receiving line has disbanded. In either case, after the beverages for the toast have been served, the wedding party waits for the speeches to begin.

Master of Ceremonies

After the wedding meal, the Master of Ceremonies is responsible for assuring that events proceed in an orderly manner. He is responsible for seeing that all toasts and speeches tie together, and that there are no large time gaps in the program. If there is an orchestra or band present, he is responsible for asking that a few bars be played to get everyone's attention, after which the toasting may begin. Often the best man acts as Master of Ceremonies, a "natural" role since he often proposes the first toast.

Etiquette

When the bride and groom are being toasted, they do not drink along with everyone else, but wait until all the others have sipped. An engaged girl or bride should always return her husband's or fiancé's toast.

It has always been common at weddings and rehearsal dinners for men to do the toasting, but it is now also considered proper for women to toast as well, if they want to do so. The suggested sequence below for formal toasting includes various responses by men on behalf of the female members of the wedding party, but of course the women are welcome to respond personally. If the bride is ill at east on her feet but needs to propose a toast, it is appropriate for her to make a very brief one, such as "I'm not good at speeches, but I would like all of you to join me in a toast to the most wonderful man in the world, my future husband."

Sequence of Toasts

The suggestions below apply to "formal" toasts. Regional customs vary, but there is almost always an event connected with the wedding during which a formal toast is in order. Of course, there are many occasions when a simple "To your health!" is appropriate, but these are mostly informal occasions when speech-making is out of place.

Although wedding protocol is not nearly as rigid today as in former times, the following "traditional" toasting order is recommended for formal toasting:

Toast to the Bride — The toast to the bride is usually made by a friend of her family, a relative, or by the best man. The person proposing the toast is introduced beforehand by the Master of Ceremonies.

This toast should not simply be a wish for happiness. It is appropriate to recount amusing anecdotes about the bride, preferably ones which provide unique insight into her personal life (perhaps some mischievous deed she did as a child, or her idiosyncratic ways of doing things). Avoid being overly sentimental, and never, never embarass the bride!

61

Toast to the Bride and Groom — Recently it has become common to include the groom in the toast to the bride, and it is also permitted to toast each of them separately at first, and then together.

When toasting both bride and groom, speak first about each of them as individuals, then about them as a couple. It is appropriate to relate personal knowledge of the relationship between their two families, as well as information about how the couple met and about their courtship. If the speaker had a role in their romance, this should of course be mentioned.

It is also appropriate to mention any outstanding special interests held by either bride or groom of which you are aware. Make sure all remarks are in good taste.

Give equal time to both families, even if the toast is to the bride only, but try to limit yourself to five minutes or less total. A toast is not the place for a lengthy family history.

Conclude your remarks by proposing a formal toast. It is customary to say, "And now, ladies and gentlemen, may I ask you to join me in wishing the charming couple health and happiness. To (bride's name) and (groom's name)!" The audience will respond, "To (bride's name) and (groom's name)," during which their glasses should be raised. Then everyone presents sips the contents of his or her glass.

If the toast is made to the bride only, the groom should stand and toast her along with everyone else, but if the toast is to both bride and groom, then both should remain seated together, smiling pleasantly. The bride and groom should never toast themselves!

Groom's Response — It is appropriate during this toast to mention by name everyone in the wedding party. It is normal to begin by making complimentary remarks about the bride, and then about the person who has just proposed the toast to the bride and groom. It is very important also

62

for the groom to thank his parents and the bride's parents, the new in-laws, the bridesmaids, and the best man during this toast.

Traditional wedding etiquette makes no provision for a speech or toast by the bride, but there is no reason she cannot say a few words at this point in the celebration. It would be appropriate for her to thank the guests for attending and for their gifts, and she may also want to express her thanks to her parents and to the groom's parents.

Best Man's Response — If the groom has proposed a toast to the bridesmaids, then the best man should respond on their behalf, adding a few complimentary remarks and expressing thanks. However, if the groom has not proposed a toast to the bridesmaids, then it is up to the best man to do so. Any other toasts that may have been omitted may also be proposed at this time, either by the best man or by someone else immediately after the best man's response.

Toast by the Father of the Bride — This is traditionally the final toast. After being introduced by the Master of Ceremonies, the bride's father thanks the guests in his and his wife's name, and also usually says something flattering about his own wife. He then makes complimentary remarks about his new in-laws, welcoming them into the family.

As the host of the party, it is the bride's father who proposes a toast to the members of the wedding party and to the guests, to which everyone in attendance can respond in unison. He then invites everyone to continue the celebration in the same spirit in which it began.

Concluding Remarks — After the bride's father has given the final toast, the Master of Ceremonies reads any telegrams which have been sent by family members or guests who were unable to attend. If these messages are witty, they will add much to the spirit of the occasion.

Second Marriages

Toasts are just as welcome at second marriages as at first marriages, although certain traditions can be ignored when both bride and groom have married before. It is appropriate for anyone to propose a toast under such circumstances, and although it is acceptable to mention any children from a previous marriage, it is in very poor taste to mention either of the bridal couple's previous marriages.

Engagement Toasts

Many times during an engagement party the father of the bride-to-be will propose an engagement toast. If toasting at a cocktail party, he should do so as soon as all the guests have arrived. At a dinner party, he may either propose his toast after everyone is seated or wait until dessert is served. Any beverage is appropriate for this toast except coffee, tea, or water.

It is quite acceptable to make a very brief toast, such as: "Will you all join me in a toast to (bride's name) and (groom's name)." Everyone then rises and drinks some of his or her beverage. The bride-and-groom-to-be remain seated until afterwards, when the groom should rise and thank the bride's father briefly.

Other toasts are unnecessary, but if anyone else wishes to propose a toast it is certainly proper to do so.

6

Sample Toasts

Sample Toasts

Helpful Hints

At one time or another almost everyone is called upon to propose a toast at a wedding. In the absence of any formal training in public speaking, many people feel ill at ease at such times. The following hints may prove useful.

1. *Be prepared.* There is no substitute for planning and foresight. Know what you will say before your turn to speak comes, and know also how you will end your speech.

2. *Use quotations.* Quotations will enrich your remarks, and will also provide words of wisdom from famous and notable persons. There are many good sources for quotations — see Chapter 7 of this book, or a standard reference work such as *Bartlett's Familiar Quotations* or the *Oxford Dictionary of Quotations.*

3. *Know your audience.* It is very likely that your audience will be quite mixed with respect to age, background, and education. Sometimes the only thing they all have in common is their acquaintance with or relation to the bridal couple.

4. *Avoid cliches.* It is better to speak "from the heart" in an original manner than to repeat a worn-out expression. Be sincere, and speak with honest affection. Eloquence is fine, if you are an experienced public speaker, but it is not essential.

5. *Be witty, but not vulgar.* It is appropriate to include jokes and witticisms in your speech as long as they do not detract from the main message or sentiment you are trying to deliver. Select your jokes with care, and avoid those that are of an ethnic or religious nature. Off-color jokes are of course taboo, as are "sick" jokes.

6. *Do not memorize your remarks.* Note cards are the best way to insure that you do not forget what you have planned to say. It does not matter if you occasionally need to refer to your notes during your speech, but you should avoid reading your presentation word-for-word. Reading means that your head is down, and you will lose eye contact with your audience. Place your cards at arm's length, just below the microphone, where you can glance at them without moving your head or straining your eyes.

7. *Do not eat or drink to excess prior to your speech.* Even if your overindulgence is not apparent to the audience, you will be more comfortable and will make a better presentation if you practice moderation.

8. *Be familiar with the microphone.* Remember that a microphone will "hear" every noise you make; thus, noisy jewelry, nervous finger tapping, and the like will be a major distraction for your audience. Also, note cards are better than crinkly stationery for your notes for this reason. Speak in a normal voice, about one-third slower than usual. Enunciate clearly, and vary your pitch so that you avoid coming across in a monotonous manner.

9. *Be sure to pronounce all names correctly.* If you are uncertain about how to pronounce anyone's name, discreetly consult a member of the wedding party or the master of ceremonies in advance.

SAMPLE TOASTS

The toasts that follow are only general suggestions with regard to format and content, and should not be used verbatim. Like any example, these "generic toasts" are rather impersonal, and should be personalized with anecdotes, quips, and so forth before they are used. Also, they are written with a view to being used at a formal reception *after* the ceremony. If formal toasting occurs instead *before* the ceremony (perhaps at the rehearsal dinner), it will be necessary to substitute "bride" for "wife" in the examples below.

Toast to the Bride

It is my honor to have been asked to propose a toast to the bride. I am delighted to do this, especially since I have known (bride's name) for quite some time.

Our bride has beauty, charm, intelligence, and many other assets that have endeared her to her family and friends. Her handsome groom is also endowed with many outstanding qualities. They share a large measure of exquisite good taste, which they have demonstrated once again by choosing each other. I know that they will spare no effort to make their marriage succeed. They are both special people who, by inviting us here today, have given us a special opportunity to participate in the celebration of their love.

Ladies and gentlemen, please join me in the traditional toast to the bride: health, happiness, and all the best that life has to offer. To (bride's name)!

Toast to the Bride

If a long association with the bride constitutes the right to propose a toast to her health and happiness, then certainly I qualify. It has been my pleasure to know (bride's name) for virtually all her life, and no one is more delighted than I to see her marry (groom's name), who seems to have all the qualities for which she has been looking.

69

May the love and affection that surround you today accompany you throughout your married life. Let me wish you a long and happy life, with the silver and gold anniversaries just around the corner. Ladies and gentlemen, please join me in a toast to the bride, for I know you feel as I do. To (bride's name)!

Toast to the Bride

This is a particularly happy moment for me. Having been asked to propose a toast to the bride, who today looks more beautiful than ever, I began to think of all her good qualities. Apart from being considerate, kind, and a loyal friend, it has always come easily to her to say things that make people feel good.

I would like to tell you all how wonderful I feel to be here, and I expect you, honored guests, to respond heartily when I say: here's to the health and happiness of (bride's name), today and always!

Toast to Bride and Groom

Ladies and gentlemen: I am not an experienced speaker, so after I consented to propose a toast to our lovely bride, I thought that the best thing to do would be to research the origin of the ritual I had been asked to perform.

The custom of drinking to the health of the bride probably started with the Greeks and Romans, and later spread to Europe. It was not until the reign of Charles II in England, however, that the custom became popular. Toasts have in the past been drunk from a lady's slipper, with the toastmaster kneeling before her or standing on a chair with one foot on the table. Fortunately, my task is simpler: I can remain standing on both feet, raise my glass, and ask this distinguished assembly to join me in a toast to the lovely bride and her handsome groom. To (bride's name) and (groom's name)!

Toast to the Bride and Groom

"God creates new worlds each day by causing marriages to take place." These words, taken from a 14th century collection of teachings on Jewish mysticism, are as significant today as when they were first written. Many cynics today look upon the traditional marriage ceremony as a meaningless ritual; happily, (bride's name) and (groom's name) have allowed God to create a new world for them today by publicly and in His presence declaring their love for each other, and by doing so they also strengthened their bond of marriage.

The wedding ceremony is more than words that are read and spoken. It is a dramatic pageant in which movement and many symbols are used to communicate the couple's feelings for each other. It leaves us looking down a road that can lead to endless joy. No doubt, there will also be hardships and difficulties along that road, and to travel it will require intelligence and discipline. Much that is ahead is uncertain, but a few things can be depended upon — faith, hope, and mutual trust. Both (bride's name) and (groom's name) can confidently set out on this road because you have all three in your hearts.

A bride and groom bring to their marriage cultural and religious heritages that will influence how they think, feel, and act toward each other. I believe that (bride's name) and (groom's name) are two well-adjusted young people who are willing to take the risks of revealing themselves meaningfully to each other, finding a style of marriage that will work for them. I am happy to propose their health to this assembly. To (bride's name) and (groom's name)!

Toast to the Bride and Groom

First, let me thank (bride's name) and (groom's name) for asking me to propose this traditional wedding toast, which I wish to address to both of them. It not only gives me a chance to tell both of you how pleased I am that you have chosen each other, it also affords me a perfect opportunity to speak a word or two about marriage.

71

Until now, I thought that the only justifiable marriage was the one that produced me. Why have I changed my mind? Why do I approve of this particular union? Because, as a personal friend of them both, I have seen these two in action. Two people who can laugh at each other's jokes, and accept with so much good humor each other's imperfections, is rare indeed. Not only can these two accept each other's flaws, they have in fact learned to love them! By doing so, they have given each other a rare and precious gift — the right to be themselves.

Ladies and gentlemen, as we raise our glasses to wish them well, let us remember how privileged we are to participate in the opening scene of what promises to be a beautiful story, played out with love and affection on the stage of life. To (bride's name) and (groom's name)!

Toast to the Bride and Groom

When I was asked to propose a toast to the bride and groom, I assumed that, in addition to expressing my good wishes, I would be expected to offer some good advice from the vast storehouse of my experience. But knowing them as two wonderful and intelligent people, I began to wonder whether they really needed my words of wisdom. After all, I got married many years ago, when the respective roles of husband and wife were much clearer, and the remarks at a wedding reception would be considered sexist by today's standards.

I believe that before (bride's name) and (groom's name) announced their intentions to marry, they already had a pretty good idea of what to expect. But there are no guarantees of success, and the two partners come to it with no more than their dreams and expectations.

Half a century ago, a famous psychologist predicted that marriage as he knew it would not last beyond 1977. Here we are, nine years later, and ninety percent of the population still finds the institution of marriage appealing. Why? Granted, it has become more flexible, emphasizing mutual support, but there seems to be no substitute for a stable and committed relationship.

I know that (bride's name) and (groom's name) care deeply about their relationship, and want it to grow and flourish. We who have come to witness their exchange of vows can but wish them well. May I ask this distinguished assembly to rise as I propost a toast to the fulfillment of their dreams and expectations. To (bride's name) and (groom's name).

Toast to the Bride and Groom

In order to do justice to this pleasant task, I shunned no effort to make this toast very special, because the two people I wish to honor are very special. To be certain of flawless delivery, I consulted famous orators, and to give substance to my remarks I consulted the most renowned men and women of letters to help me phrase my good wishes. However, in the end I felt compelled to say, in my own way, the things that are closest to my heart.

I have known (bride's name) and (groom's name) for a number of years, and we are good friends. Early on in their friendship, I was able to see that it was developing into something lasting. When they decided to build a life together, I knew that marriage would be a rewarding experience for them.

As their good friend, I suppose it falls to me to offer at least one piece of advice, which I will do by saying simply that marriage is always a cooperative effort. The point is not to determine who is right or wrong at any moment. It is not true that one wins when the other loses, for if one loses both lose. May you both be winners!

Friends, let us wish these two fortunate people many wonderful things as they start life together. Please rise and join me in a toast to their good health and happiness! To (bride's name) and (groom's name)!

Toast to the Bride and Groom

I believe that brevity is the soul of wit, and as such I promise to make a very witty speech indeed. I have known the bride and groom for a very long time, and I was quite honored when they asked me to say a few words today.

If it hadn't been for me, these two would probably never have met, and when they did meet I did my best to encourage their relationship, probably to the detriment of my own social life. For look at me — it is they who are married, and not I! Like most married people, they will probably try to fix me up with someone, telling me it's for my own good. So be it!

True to my promise to be brief, I now wish to propose a toast to the continued happiness and health of my good friends, (bride's name) and (groom's name).

Response by the Groom

Mr. (toaster's name), honored guests, my wife and I are honored by the wonderful way you have honored us on our special day. We thank you for your enthusiastic response to the good wishes expressed by our friend.

I know that everything he said about (bride's name) is true, but I was overwhelmed by his remarks about me. I cannot help but wonder if I am worthy of such praise, and I know that I shall have to set high standards for myself to live up to it.

I also want to thank (bride's name)'s mother and father, Mr. and Mrs. (bride's parents' name), for the way they have accepted me into their family as their new son. I shall do my best not to disappoint them, and I promise to be a good husband to (bride's name).

Special thanks are in order to my own parents, who have always supported me in all my endeavors. I know I shall profit by the example they set as husband and wife. They have provided an excellent example of a good marriage.

I thank our guests for their generosity, and in return my wife and I offer you our hospitality. Thank you again for your thoughtfulness and good wishes.

Response by the Groom

Ladies and gentlemen, I must confess that (toaster's name) makes me somewhat uneasy by saying all those wonderful things about us. I know that my lovely bride deserves them, but do I? To live up to this kind of tribute, I shall have to mend my ways!

74

I would like to thank (bride's name) for consenting to become my wife. I also want to thank her mother and father for entrusting her to my care. To my own parents, I say: thank you for your love and understanding. You have never failed to support any of my endeavors, odd as they may have seemed at times.

Nothing is as cheerful as the wholehearted support of family and friends. By being here and sharing this wonderful occasion with us, you have helped us get off to the right start. The lovely gifts you have given us, and the many good wishes that went with them, will be a constant reminder of your kindness. My wife joins me in thanking you for your kindness and generosity.

Response by the Groom

Ladies and gentlemen, I thank you for your kind words and for all your good wishes, coming as they do from good friends and members of both families. Your friendship and affection will no doubt assist us in meeting any adversity with confidence.

In thanking you for sharing this wonderful day with us, my wife and I also want to express our gratitude to our immediate families, the bridesmaids, and the best man. You have helped make this day one we will cherish for the rest of our lives.

Response by the Groom, with a Toast

My wife and I wish to thank (toaster's name) for the wonderful way he proposed the toast to my lovely bride. His good wishes make us both very happy. We are also delighted that all of you have been able to share this special day with us.

I would like to express sincere thanks to a few special people — my new in-laws, my own mother and father, the bridesmaids, and of course the best man. All of you have contributed to making this day so memorable. I propose a toast to you, and to my lovely bride as well. To (bride's name)!

Response by the Groom, with a Toast

Ladies and gentlemen, first of all my wife and I would like to thank (toaster's name) for his kind words and good wishes. To our honored guests, I express my thanks for responding with so much enthusiasm and good humor. I also thank you for the generous gifts you have given us, and I sincerely hope you will visit our new home soon to see them.

A very special thank-you goes to my new in-laws, Mr. and Mrs. (in-laws' name), who have not only entrusted me with their daughter but also have spared no effort to make this celebration both memorable and meaningful.

I would like to propose a toast to them, as well as to my own mother and father, and also to the bridesmaids. To Mr. and Mrs. (in-laws' name), to Mom and Dad, and to (bridesmaids' names).

Groom's Response, with Toast to Bridesmaids

Distinguished guests, we thank you for your kind words, which touched us deeply. We appreciate your confidence in our ability to make a successful marriage. We have love and mutual trust to guide us, but any advice from one more experienced in marriage is always welcome.

My beautiful bride has accepted me with all my weaknesses, and I thank her for it. I have not so far found any in her, but if I do I promise to accept them with tact and understanding.

My task would not be complete without expressing sincere thanks to Mr. and Mrs. (in-laws' name), my new in-laws, who accepted me with so much kindness. To my own mother and father I say: thank you for all your love and devotion, which gave me the security and confidence to love and cherish my new wife, (bride's name).

I also want to tell our honored guests how much their presence here today means to us. My final word of thanks goes to the bridesmaids, whose dedication to their jobs was unsurpassed. I propose a toast to their good health and happiness. To (bridesmaids' names).

Groom's Response, with Toast to Bridesmaids

Ladies and gentlemen, my wife and I thank you for the good wishes you have expressed to us on this occasion. I am very happy today, and when I look at (bride's name), she looks lovelier than ever, which may be due in part to her own happiness.

I would also like to thank (bridesmaids' names), whose efforts and infinite skill helped make this day go so well. Please join me in drinking a toast to their health and happiness. To (bridesmaids' names).

Best Man's Toast to the Bridesmaids

Ladies and gentlemen, it is now my pleasure to propose a toast to the good health of the bridesmaids. So far all the attention has been focused on these two happy people — the bride and groom — but I know I speak for them when I say that they will not mind if some of the glory goes to these delightful ladies, who have done more than their share to make this day such a great success.

Without further ado, let me thank them and ask you to join me in a toast to (bridesmaids' names).

Best Man's Toast to the Bridesmaids

Today it has not only been my pleasant duty to attend to the bridegroom's every need, I also was asked to look after the bridesmaids. The latter proved to be a very simple task because they very ably took care of themselves.

Once the ceremony was over and my friend was safely married, I thought that there would be nothing more for me to do. Now, however, I realize that I would be remiss in my duty if I did not thank the bridesmaids for performing so splendidly at our friends' wedding, and I hasten to propose a toast to them. To (bridesmaids' names).

Best Man's Response to a Toast to the Bridesmaids Proposed by the Groom

In response to my good friend's toast to the bridesmaids, I

would like to thank him on their behalf for all the nice things he said about them. I think they are the best bridesmaids I have ever encountered at all the weddings I have been to lately.

I would like to add my good wishes to the happy couple, and I know the bridesmaids, (bridesmaids' names), would want me to include theirs also.

Toast by the Father of the Bride

This is a joyful occasion, and it has turned out to be a very happy day for all of us. My wife and I wish to thank you for joining us to celebrate the marriage of our beautiful daughter, (bride's name), to (groom's name), our new son-in-law.

We have known many of you for quite some time, and we hope that those among you whom we have only recently met will become our good friends, especially (groom's name)'s family and friends.

I would like to propose a toast to you, our honored guests, to wish you joy and happiness. To you!

Toast by the Father of the Bride

What greater reward can a father expect than to see his daughter as happy as (bride's name) is today? If possible, the only greater happiness is that my wife and I have been able to share our happiness this day with you, our honored guests. Your presence here today has been very special to us, and we thank you.

I would like to propose a toast to our wonderful guests. Here's to your health, and may you all live long and prosper.

Second Marriage Toast to Bride and Groom

There must be something truly extraordinary about marriage, since more and more people are finding it appealing. To be married is a special event; to be married a second time is an even greater step, and calls for a very special celebration. Both of you are more mature and perhaps a bit less idealistic than the first time, though you will still have to learn to adjust to each other just like all newlyweds do.

You are both aware of the pitfalls of married life, and thus are in a good position to avoid them. You will of course make mistakes, but that is only human. There will be new problems to solve, new decisions to make, and new solutions to discover. I know you will both approach the task with love and dedication.

Dr. Samuel Johnson called second marriage "the triumph of hope over experience." Ladies and gentlemen, may I ask you to join me in a toast to the happy couple. To (bride's name) and (groom's name) — good health and happiness for a long and prosperous life!

Toast Notes

Toast Notes

Toast Notes

7

Quotes

Quotes

When proposing toasts, it is often desirable to make reference to one or more quotations from famous persons. The following pages list some appropriate quotations for wedding toasts. Your local book store or library will have many sources of such material.

"Love does not consist in gazing at each other, but in looking outward in the same direction." — Antoine de Saint-Exupery

"There is no remedy for love than to love more."
— Henry David Thoreau

"When there's room in the heart there is room in the house."
— Danish Proverb

"Laughter is the sunshine of the soul."
— Ralph Waldo Emerson

"To be prepared is half the victory."   — Cervantes

"What is not good for the hive is not good for the bee."
— Marcus Aurelius

"If there is such a thing as a good marriage, it is because it resembles friendship rather than love."
— Michel E. de Montaigne

"Happiness in marriage is entirely a matter of chance."
— Jane Austen

"A man's friendships are, like his will, invalidated by marriage — but they are also no less invalidated by the marriage of his friends."   — Samuel Butler

"One should believe in marriage as in the immortality of the soul."   — Honore de Balzac

"The greatest happiness of life is the conviction that we are loved, loved for ourselves, or rather loved in spite of ourselves."   — Victor Marie Hugo

"The only gift is a portion of thyself."
                                        — Ralph Waldo Emerson

"Here's to marriage, that happy estate that resembles a pair of scissors: 'So joined that they cannot be separated, often moving in opposite directions, yet punishing anyone who comes between them.'"   — Sydney Smith

"Thinking is easy, action is difficult; to act in accordance with one's thoughts is the most difficult thing in the world."
                                        — Johann Wolfgang von Goethe

"To be wronged is nothing unless you continue to remember it."   — Confucius

"A wife is essential for longevity; she is the receptacle of half a man's cares and two-thirds of his ill humor."
                                        — Charles Reade

"We judge ourselves by what we feel capable of doing, while others judge us by what we have already done."
                                        — Henry Wadsworth Longfellow

"To be loved, be lovable."   — Ovid

"Keep your eyes wide open before marriage, half shut afterwards." — Benjamin Franklin

"Here's to you as good as you are,
And here's to me, as bad as I am;
As bad as I am, as good as you are,
I'm as good as you are as bad as I am." — Old Scottish Toast

"May your joys be as deep as the ocean, and your sorrows as light as its foam." — Anonymous

"The great secret of successful marriage is to treat all disasters as incidents and none of the incidents as disasters." — Harold Nicholson

"Spend more imagination than money." — Lyndon B. Johnson

"Those marriages generally abound most with love and constancy that are preceded by a long courtship." — Joseph Addison

"When a match has equal partners, then I fear not." — Aeschylus

"Marriage, to woman as to men, must be a luxury, not a necessity; an incident of life, not all of it." — Susan B. Anthony

"Where there's marriage without love, there will be love without marriage." — Benjamin Franklin

"Let there be space in your togetherness." — Kahlil Gibran

"There is no more lovely, friendly, and charming relationship, communion, or company than a good marriage." — Martin Luther

"A good marriage is that in which each appoints the other the guardian of his solitude."　　　　　— Rainer Marie Rilke

"To marry is to halve your rights and double your duties."
　　　　　　　— Arthur Schopenhauer

"The world has grown suspicious of anything that looks like a happy married life."　　　　　— Oscar Wilde

"Beauty is the gift of God."　　　　　— Aristotle

"Beauty is in the eye of the beholder." — Margaret Hungerford

"A thing of beauty is a joy for ever:
Its loveliness increases; it will never
Pass into nothingness."　　　　　— John Keats

"'Beauty is truth, truth beauty,' — that is all Ye know on earth, and all ye need to know."　　　　　— John Keats

"A journey of a thousand miles begins with one step."
　　　　　　　— Lao Tzu

"The beginning is the most important part of the work."
　　　　　　　— Plato

"Faint heart never won fair lady."　　　　　— Cervantes

"The heart that loves is always young."　　　— Greek Proverb

"Absence makes the heart grow fonder."　　　— T. H. Bayly

"Who can give law to lovers? Love is a greater law to itself."
　　　　　　　— Boethius

"Love is blind."　　　　　— Chaucer

"All mankind love a lover."   — Ralph Waldo Emerson

"It requires far more genius to make love than to command armies."   — Ninon de Lenclos

"It is love, not reason, that is stronger than death."   — Thomas Mann

"Love is the joy of the good, the wonder of the wise, the amazement of the Gods."   — Plato

"Love means never having to say you're sorry."   — Erich Segal

"The course of true love never did run smooth."   — Shakespeare

"Let me not to the marriage of true minds
Admit impediments. Love is not love
Which alters when it alterations finds,
Or bends with the remover to remove.
Oh no! It is an ever-fixed mark
That looks on tempests and is never shaken. It is the
star to every wandering bark,
Whose worth's unknown, although his height be taken."   — Shakespeare

"One word frees us of all the weight and pain of life: That word is love."   — Sophocles

"Love conquers all: and let us too surrender to love."   — Virgil

"Love those who love you."   — Voltaire

"He that can't endure the bad will not live to see the good."   — Jewish Proverb

"No act of kindness, no matter how small, is ever wasted."
— Aesop

"Manners are the happy way of doing things."
— Ralph Waldo Emerson

WORKS CONSULTED

1. *The Amy Vanderbilt Complete Book of Etiquette,* revised edition by Letitia Baldridge. Published in 1978 by Doubleday and Co.

2. *Bartlett's Familiar Quotations* by John Bartlett, 15th edition. Published in 1980 by Little, Brown and Co.

3. *The Bride's Book of Etiquette* by the Editors of Bride's Magazine. Published in 1967 by Grossett & Dunlap.

4. *Complete Book of Roasts, Boasts and Toasts* by Elmer Pasta. Published in 1982 by Parker Publishing Co.

5. *The Complete Toastmaster* by Herbert V. Prochnow. Published in 1960 by Prentice-Hall.

6. *The Complete Wedding Planner* by Edith Gilbert. Published in 1983 by Warner Books.

7. *The Customs of Mankind* by Lillian Eichler. Published in 1924 by Nelson Doubleday.

8. *Emily Post's Complete Book of Wedding Etiquette* by Elizabeth L. Post. Published in 1982 by Harper & Row.

9. *The Encyclopedia of Christian Marriage.* Published in 1983 by Fleming H. Revell Co.

10. *The Eternal Bliss Machine* by Marcia Seligson. Published in 1973 by William Morrow and Co.

11. *Folkways* by William Graham Sumner. Published in 1959 by Dover Publications.

12. *It's Fun to Entertain* by Blackie Scott. Published in 1983 by Peachtree Publishers, Ltd.

13. *The Knight, the Lady, and the Priest* by Georges Duby. Published in 1983 by Pantheon Books.

14. *Modern Bride Guide To Your Wedding and Marriage.* Published in 1984 by Ballantine.

15. *The New International Dictionary of Quotations* by Hugh Rawson and Margaret Miner. Published in 1986 by E. P. Dutton.

16. *Something Borrowed, Something Blue* by Matilda Nordtvedt and Pearl Steinkuehler. Published in 1981 by Moody Press.

17. *Something Old, Something New* by Matilda Nordtvedt and Pearl Steinkuehler. Published in 1981 by Moody Press.

18. *Thesaurus of Anecdotes* by Edmund Fuller. Published in 1948 by Garden City Publishing Co.

19. *The Vanishing Irish* by John A. O'Brien. Published in 1953 by McGraw-Hill.

20. *The Waning of the Middle Ages* by Johan Huizinga. Published in 1954 by Doubleday Anchor Books.

21. *Wedding Anniversary Celebrations* by Beatrice Plumb, Mabel N. Fuller, et. al. Published in 1951 by T.S. Denison & Company.

22. *Wedding Toasts and How to Propose Them* by Lesley Wyle. Published in 1983 by Royce Publications, Canada.

23. *Weddings* by Emily Post. Published in 1963 by Simon and Schuster.

24. *Your Wedding: How To Plan and Enjoy It* by Marjorie Binford Woods. Published in 1977 by Jove.

Books to Make the Wedding Special

Wedding Ceremony Idea Book
by George W. Knight
More and more, couples are writing all or part of their own ceremony; this handy sourcebook helps couples add a personal touch to even the most traditional wedding. It contains six complete ceremonies and scores of suggestions for all parts of the wedding to help create a beautiful and original ceremony. Our best seller, now in its fourth printing.
    0-939298-01-5   paper   96 pages   7.95

When Your Daughter Marries
by Rayburn W. Ray and Rose Ann Ray
A survival guide for the bride's parents! Comprehensive yet concise, this volume contains numerous suggestions on how the bride's parents can plan a beautiful and affordable wedding. A step-by-step guide with a quick-reference index.
    0-939298-14-7   paper   96 pages $7.95

After You've Said I Do
by Hardy R. Denham, Jr.
A guide to the early years of marriage—including the meaning of marital love, ways to improve communication, and how to handle inevitable conflict. Not only a popular, inexpensive gift for newlyweds—but also an effective counseling guide for ministers and professional wedding counselors!
    0-939298-18-X   paper   96 pages   7.95

The Groom's Wedding Guidebook
by Rayburn and Rose Ann Ray
The Rays' companion volume to *When Your Daughter Marries* focuses distinctively on the role of the groom in planning the wedding event.
    "If you want your future husband to be calm, cool, and collected on your wedding day, this book would be a wonderful 'I love you' gift, especially for him." — *Indiana Bride*
    0-939298-22-8   paper   92 pages   7.95

The Second Marriage Guidebook
by George W. Knight
Thousands of people remarry each year; this book explains how to plan a unique and meaningful second marriage ceremony. Questions on etiquette, dress, and financing are answered. There are special sections on how to tell the children and involve them in the ceremony, and how to merge two families with their own traditions into a harmonious household.
    0-939298-23-6   paper   96 pages   7.95

Marriage Renewal Sourcebook
by Hardy R. Denham
More and more couples are enjoying the exciting experience of Marriage Renewal. This handy guide covers redefining roles, reevaluating goals, and recommitting to a relationship. As well as being an invaluable how-to guide, this book is a popular and valuable counseling tool.
    0-939298-24-4   paper   96 pages   7.95

Wedding Toasts and Traditions
by Mark Ishee
How to toast, when to toast, and what to say—together in a single volume with the often-obscure origins of various wedding traditions, customs, and superstitions. No other book provides as much information on the history and development of the modern marriage ceremony. A must for ministers, marriage consultants, and caterers—and a nice gift for the bride's (or groom's) father!
    0-939298-45-7   paper   96 pages   7.95

Wedding Anniversary Idea Book
by Rayburn and Rose Ann Ray
Ideas for celebrating wedding anniversaries, with special emphasis on the first, twenty-fifth, and fiftieth.
    "We believe that wedding anniversaries can be fun...and can provide the periods of reflection and renewal needed in every marriage. Positive anniversary events can definitely strengthen a marriage and enrich family life."
    0-939298-43-0   paper   96 pages   7.95

Bridal Shower Guidebook
by Myra M. Ishee
How often have you wanted to host a bridal shower for a friend, but have despaired of doing the "same old thing?"

The *Bridal Shower Guidebook* assists the hostess in the planning and creation of memorable showers, but it is not so much a "rule book" as an "idea book." Emphasizing practical concerns, it contains gift ideas, recipes, suggested menus, games, theme ideas, seasonal suggestions, etiquette, and guidelines for planning and hosting.

A one-of-a-kind book—which will help make your shower an original, creative occasion!

"Chock full of imaginative menus, gift ideas, and successful planning guidelines."—*Bride's* Magazine

0-939298-44-9   paper   96 pages   7.95

Financial Planning for Newlyweds
by Mike Speer
This comprehensive guide contains tips on saving money, spending and investing wisely, saving on taxes, avoiding money-management mistakes, and preparing for emergencies. A special section on setting financial goals helps newlyweds plan for the future—and realize those plans!

Financial Planning for Newlyweds is a great gift for the bride or groom— one that sets the new family on the path to a solid financial future.

0-939298-50-3   paper   128 pages   7.95